WILD ANIMAL SUDOKU

**Frank Coussement &
Peter De Schepper**

Sterling Publishing Co., Inc.
New York

10 9 8 7 6 5 4 3 2 1

Published by Sterling Publishing Co., Inc.
387 Park Avenue South, New York, NY 10016
© 2007 by Frank Coussement & Peter De Schepper
Distributed in Canada by Sterling Publishing
c/o Canadian Manda Group, 165 Dufferin Street
Toronto, Ontario, Canada M6K 3H6
Distributed in the United Kingdom by GMC Distribution Services
Castle Place, 166 High Street, Lewes, East Sussex, England BN7 1XU
Distributed in Australia by Capricorn Link (Australia) Pty. Ltd.
P.O. Box 704, Windsor, NSW 2756, Australia

Printed in China

Sterling ISBN-13: 978-1-4027-4366-5
         ISBN-10: 1-4027-4366-1

For information about custom editions, special sales, premium and
corporate purchases, please contact Sterling Special Sales
Department at 800-805-5489 or specialsales@sterlingpub.com.

Introduction

Do you like pencil puzzles and games? Are you tired of playing tic-tac-toe and hangman? If you can count from 1 to 9, then sudoku is perfect for you!

Sudoku is like a jigsaw puzzle but without all the messy pieces. Turn the page and we'll show you step-by-step how to solve an exciting sudoku puzzle. It only uses 6 numbers, but the same fun and easy steps will help you work more sudokus—with 8 and even 9 numbers!

Some of the puzzles have special clues to help you solve them faster and easier. With these colorful hints and a little practice, you will quickly become a sudoku master.

Wishing you lots of puzzle fun!

How to Solve a Sudoku

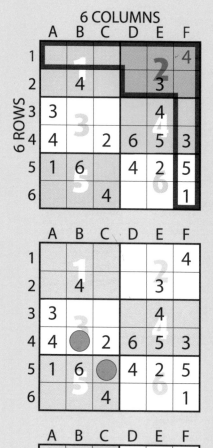

Step 1:

Fill in the grid so that each column, each row, and each frame contains every number from 1 to 6.

A 6x6 sudoku grid is divided into 6 rows, 6 columns, and 6 small frames. Every number from 1 to 6 appears in each row, column, and frame. In the drawing on the left, the blue number 4 is in row 1, in column F, and in box frame 2. This means that row 1, column F, and frame 2 cannot contain another number 4.

Step 2:

Always look for places where there are already lots of numbers. Rows 4 and 5 already have five out of the six numbers filled in, so it's easy to figure out which numbers should go in the empty spots. You can fill in number 1 in row 4 and number 3 in row 5.

Step 3:

In column E, the numbers 1 and 6 are missing. But where do the 1 and the 6 belong? Frame 6 already has a number 1, so you can't put another number 1 in that frame. But if you fill in a 6 at the bottom of column E and a 1 at the top, frame 6 is only missing one number in the red circle — the 3.

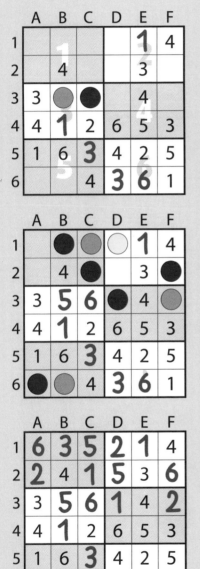

Step 4:

Now we can look for other places where only two numbers are missing. Which number belongs in the green circle of frame 3? 1, 2, 3, and 4 are already in the frame. Number 6 is in column B, so 5 is the only possible answer. Do you know which number is still missing in the red?

Step 5:

From here, you can complete the sudoku. First, fill in the missing numbers in the green circles. Then you'll know right away which numbers belong in the red circles. You're almost done! Now, fill in the number in the yellow circle. After that, you can solve the rest of the sudoku.

Step 6:

Each sudoku has a different solution.

I wish you fun and success with your first sudoku. Just turn the page.

7

SUDOKU 6X6

2	1	4	3	5	6
3	6	5	1	4	2
5	4	6	2	1	3
1	3	2	5	6	4
6	2	1	4	3	5
4	5	3	6	2	1

9

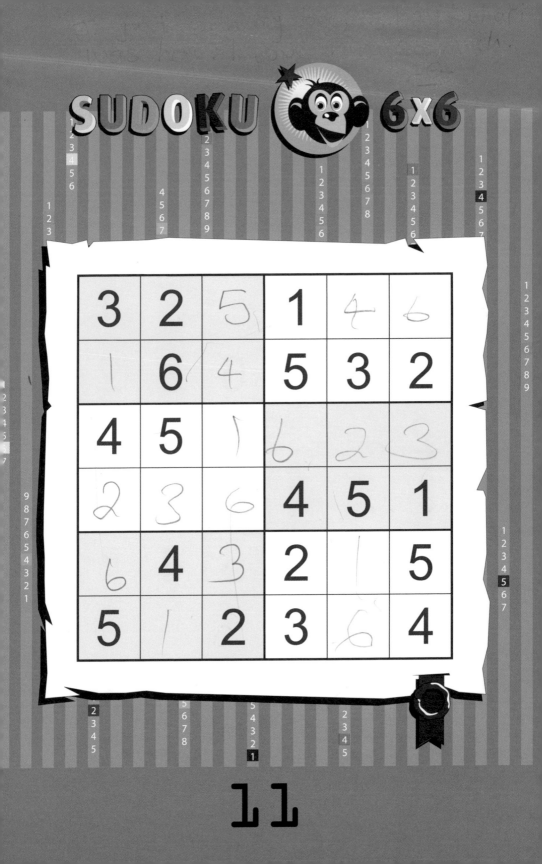

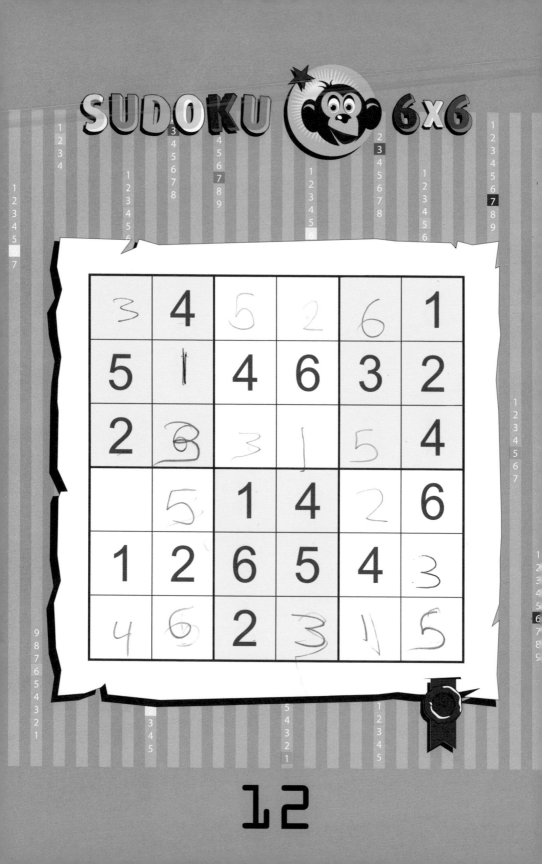

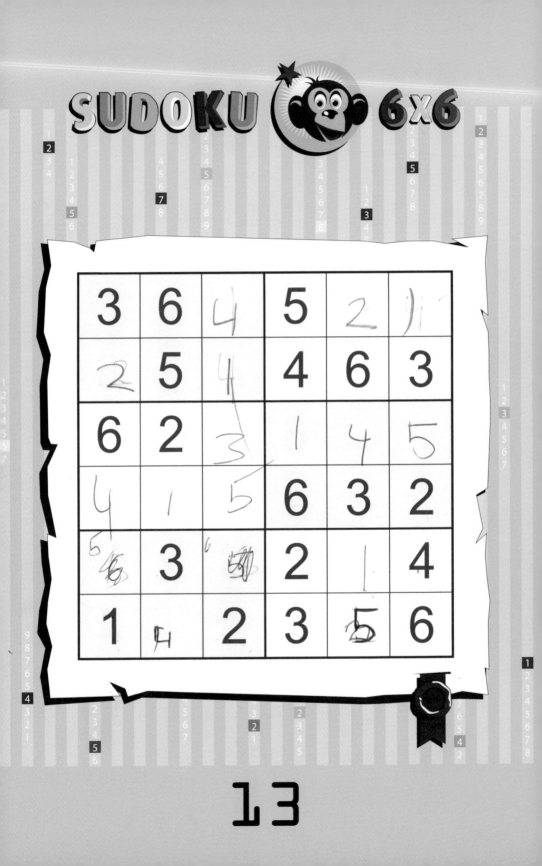

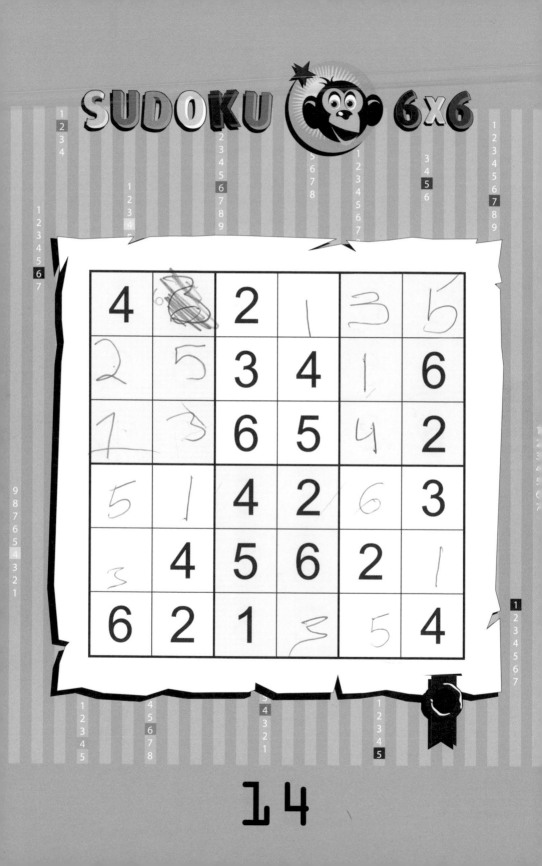

SUDOKU 6X6

14

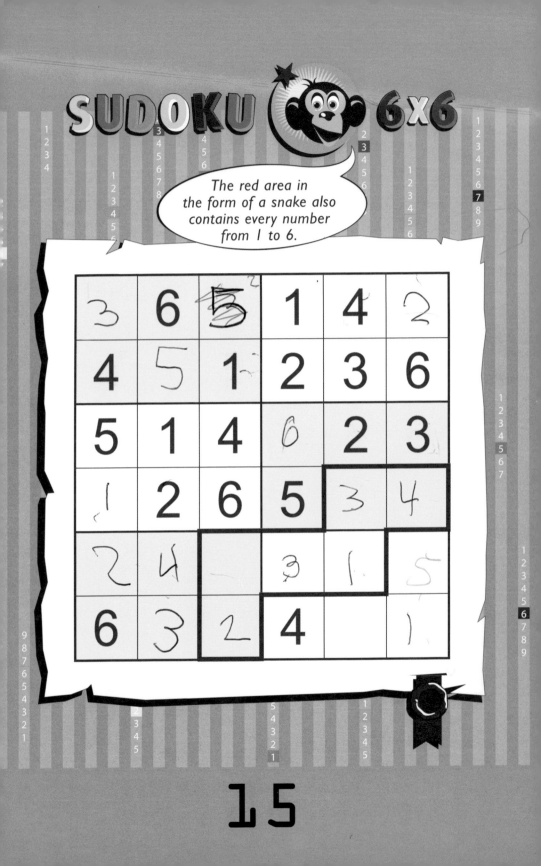

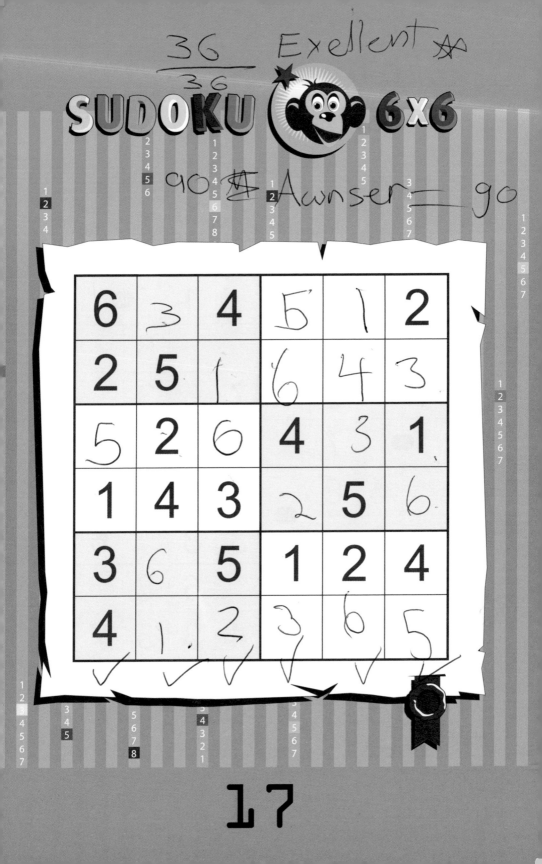

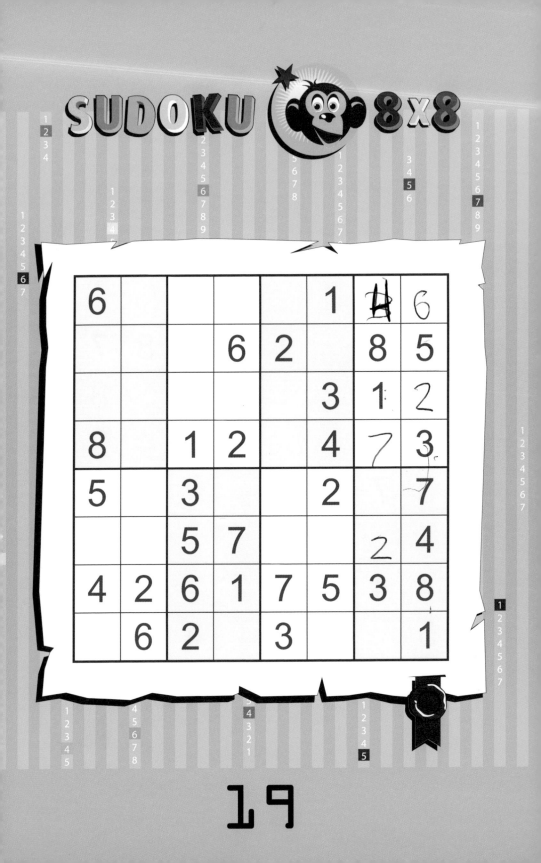

SUDOKU 8x8

	5	7			3		
	3		1	5	2	8	7
	2			7			8
8				3		4	2
3	7		4			2	
1		2				3	
7	4	3		2		5	
5		8			4		

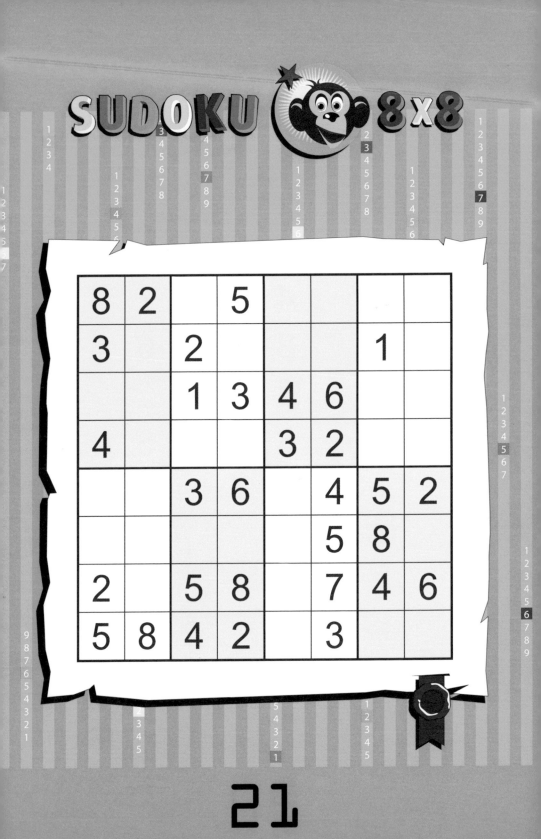

SUDOKU 8X8

21

SUDOKU 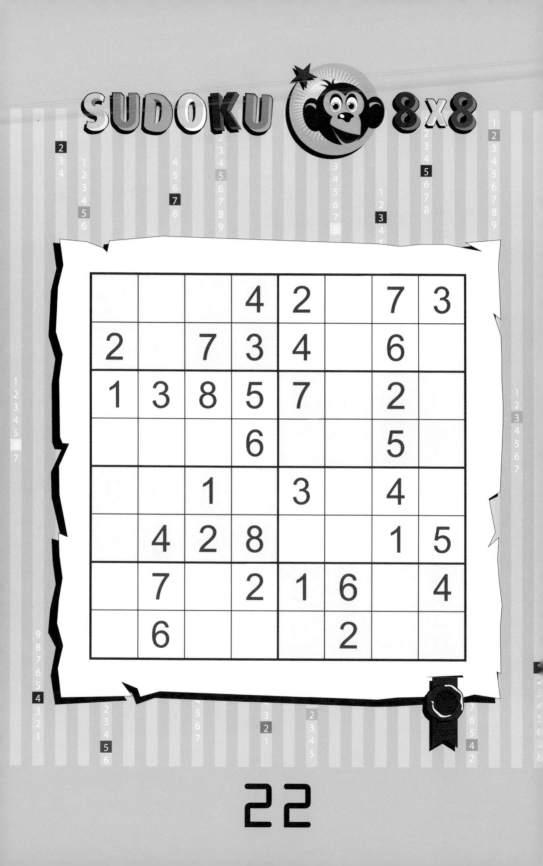 8x8

			4	2		7	3
2		7	3	4		6	
1	3	8	5	7		2	
			6			5	
		1		3		4	
	4	2	8			1	5
	7		2	1	6		4
	6				2		

22

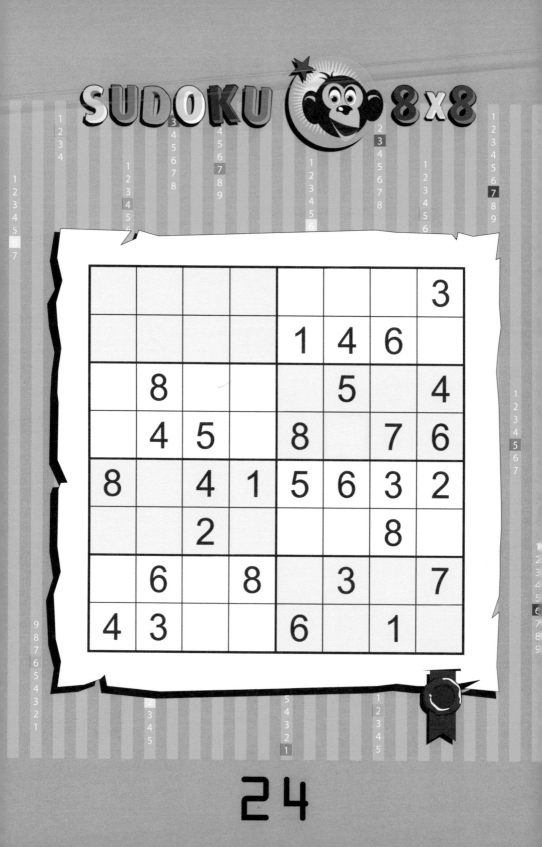

24

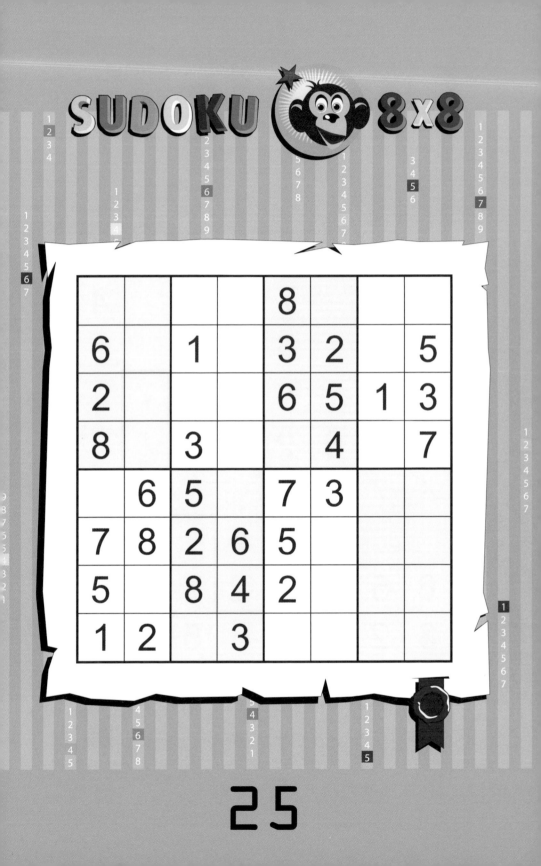

SUDOKU 8x8

				8			
6		1		3	2		5
2				6	5	1	3
8		3			4		7
	6	5		7	3		
7	8	2	6	5			
5		8	4	2			
1	2		3				

25

SUDOKU 8×8

The red area in the form of a snake also contains every number from 1 to 8.

26

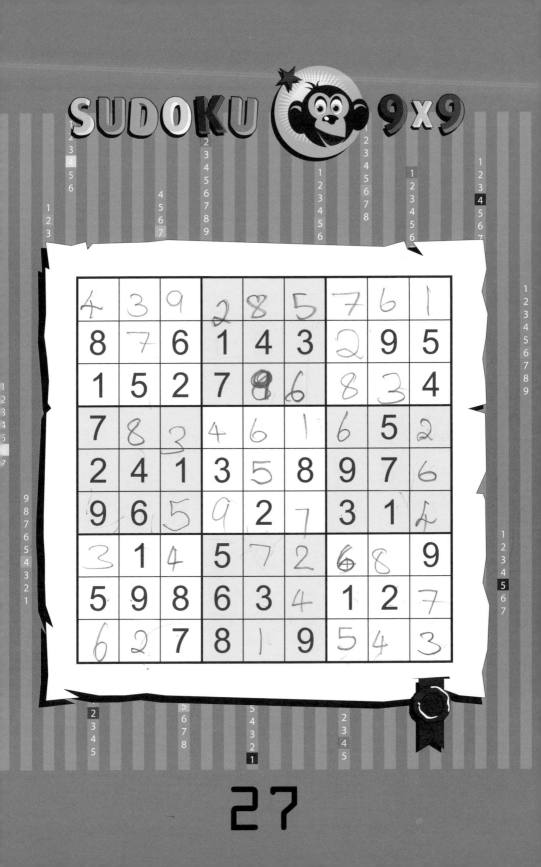

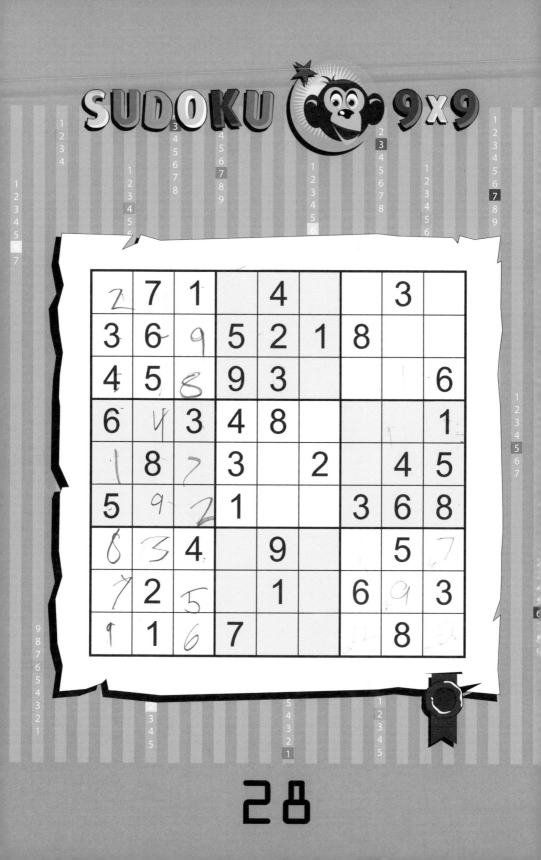

SUDOKU 9X9

2	7	1		4			3	
3	6	9	5	2	1	8		
4	5	8	9	3				6
6	4	3	4	8				1
1	8	7	3		2		4	5
5	9	2	1			3	6	8
8	3	4		9			5	7
7	2	5		1		6	9	3
9	1	6	7				8	

28

SUDOKU 9X9

3	4	6	5	7	1	8	2	9
1	9	2	8	6	4	3	7	5
7	5	8	2	9	3	4	1	6
2	7	4	1	8	9	5	6	3
6	3	5	4	2	7	1	9	8
9	8	1	3	5	6	2	4	7
5	1	9	6	3	2	7	8	4
4	6	3	7	1	8	9	5	2
8	2	7	9	4	5	6	3	1

29

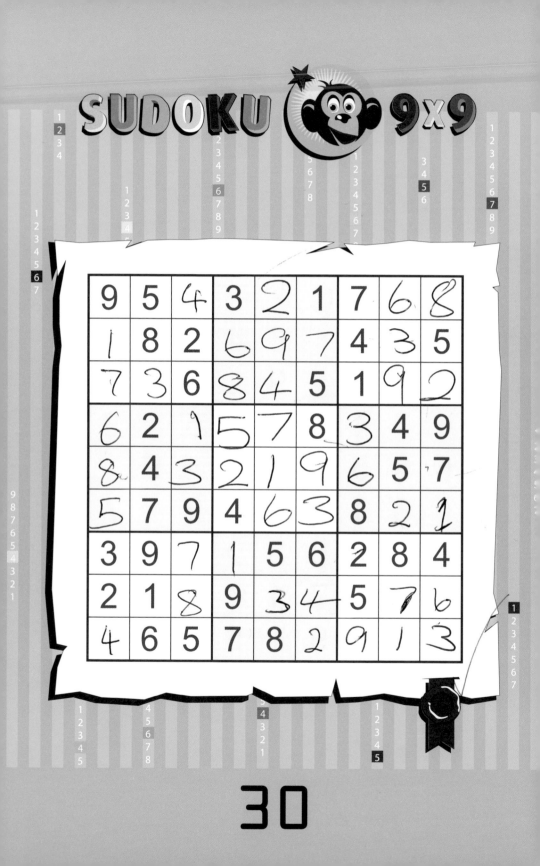

SUDOKU 9x9

9	5	4	3	2	1	7	6	8
1	8	2	6	9	7	4	3	5
7	3	6	8	4	5	1	9	2
6	2	1	5	7	8	3	4	9
8	4	3	2	1	9	6	5	7
5	7	9	4	6	3	8	2	1
3	9	7	1	5	6	2	8	4
2	1	8	9	3	4	5	7	6
4	6	5	7	8	2	9	1	3

30

Contents

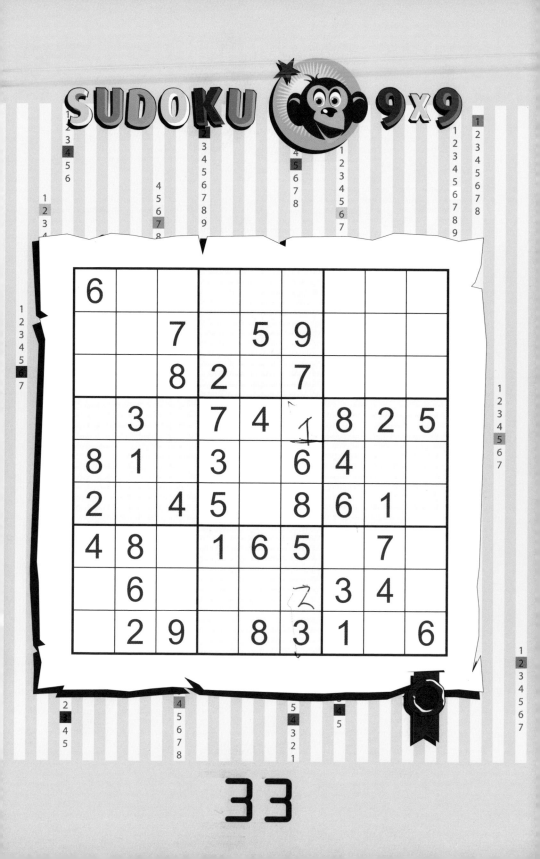

SUDOKU 9x9

33

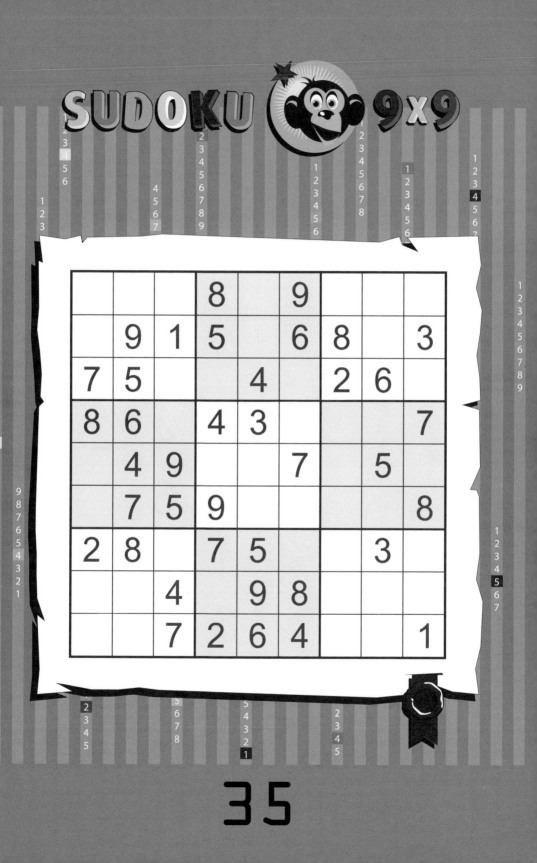

SUDOKU 9x9

35

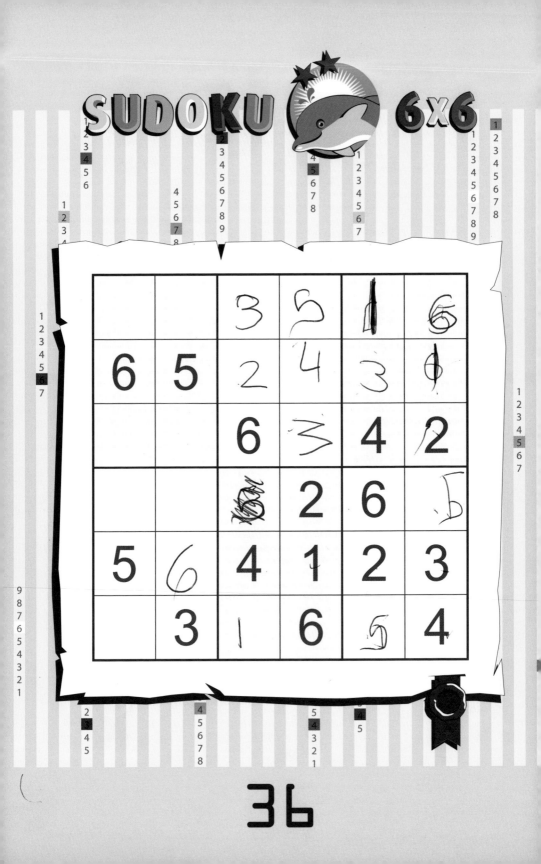

SUDOKU 6x6

36

SUDOKU 6X6

3	1	6	5	4	2
4	5	2	1	3	6
1	6	4	3	2	5
5	2	3	6	1	4
6	4	1	2	5	3
2	3	5	4	6	1

37

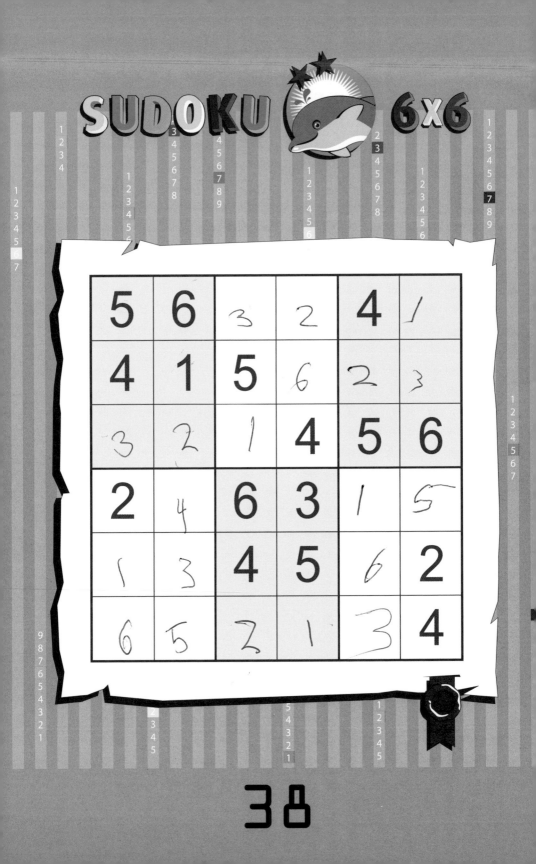

SUDOKU 6x6

The red area in the form of a snake also contains every number from 1 to 6.

1	6	2	5	3	4
3	5	4	1	6	2
6	4	3	2	5	1
2	1	5	6	4	3
5	3	1	4	2	6
4	2	6	3	1	5

39

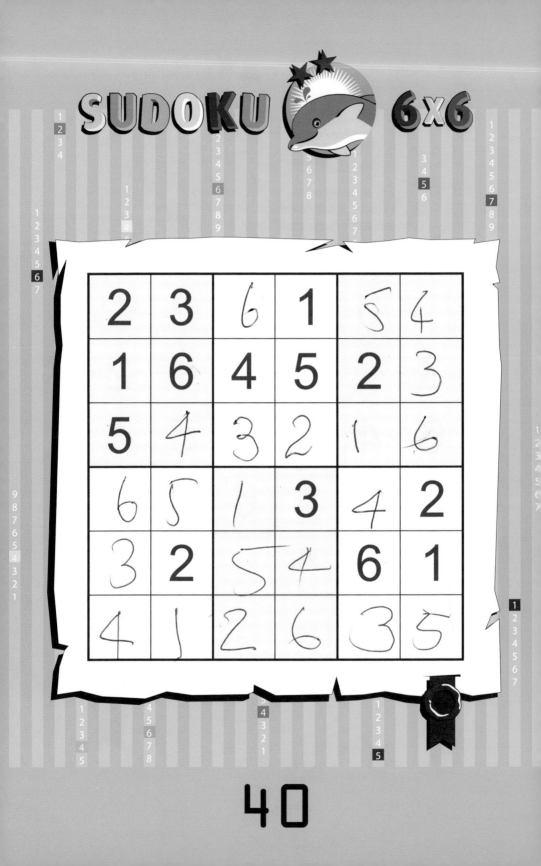

SUDOKU 6X6

2	3	6	1	5	4
1	6	4	5	2	3
5	4	3	2	1	6
6	5	1	3	4	2
3	2	5	4	6	1
4	1	2	6	3	5

40

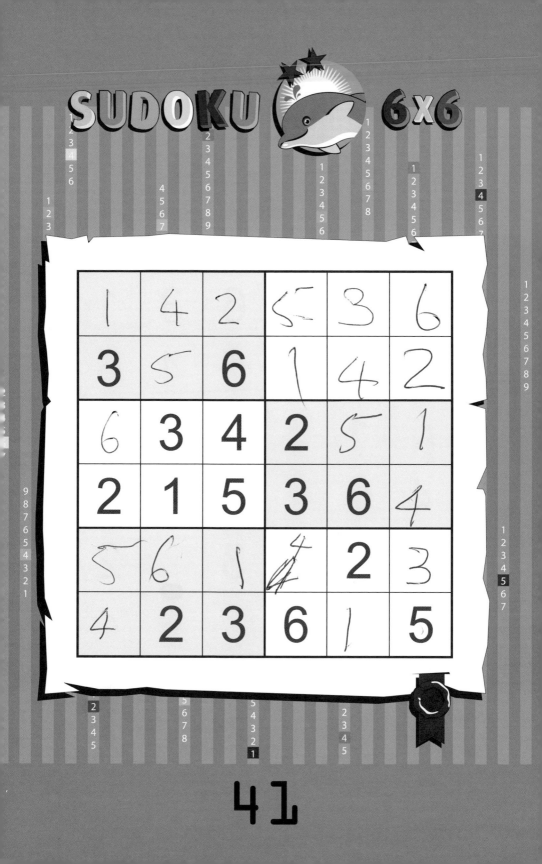

SUDOKU 6x6

1	4	2	5	3	6
3	5	6	1	4	2
6	3	4	2	5	1
2	1	5	3	6	4
5	6	1	4	2	3
4	2	3	6	1	5

41

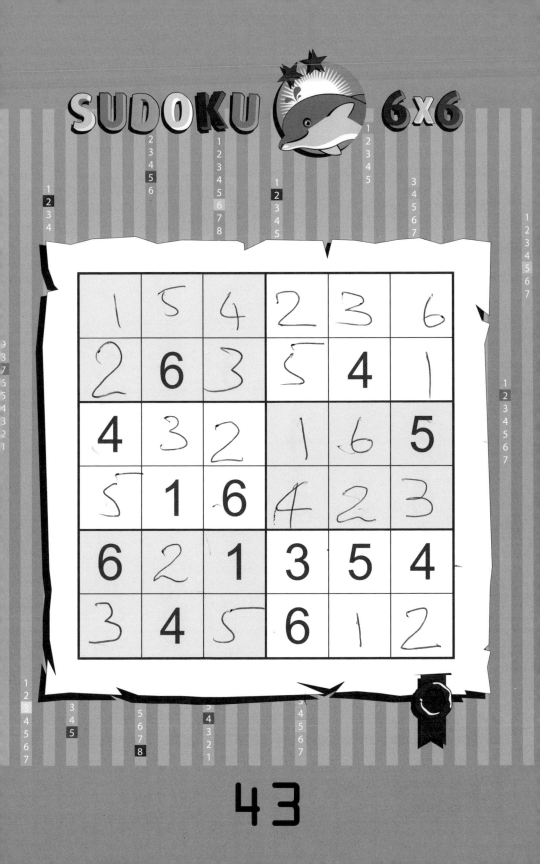

SUDOKU 6X6

1	5	4	2	3	6
2	6	3	5	4	1
4	3	2	1	6	5
5	1	6	4	2	3
6	2	1	3	5	4
3	4	5	6	1	2

43

SUDOKU 6x6

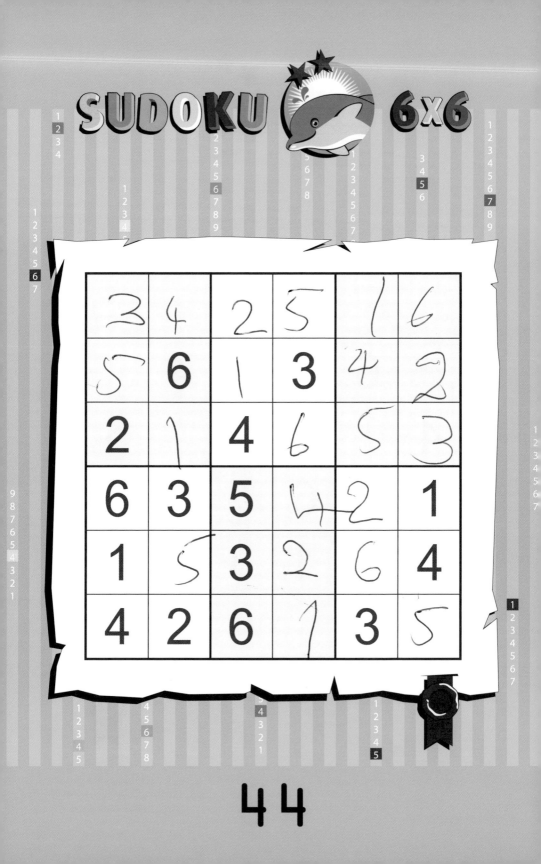

3	4	2	5	1	6
5	6	1	3	4	2
2	1	4	6	5	3
6	3	5	4	2	1
1	5	3	2	6	4
4	2	6	1	3	5

44

SUDOKU 8x8

6	1	2	3	5	7	8	4
2	4	8	7	6	3	1	5
3	8	5	1	4	2	6	7
7	5	6	4	8	1	2	3
4	7	3	6	2	8	5	1
1	6	4	2	7	5	3	8
8	3	7	5	1	6	4	2
5	2	1	8	3	4	7	6

45

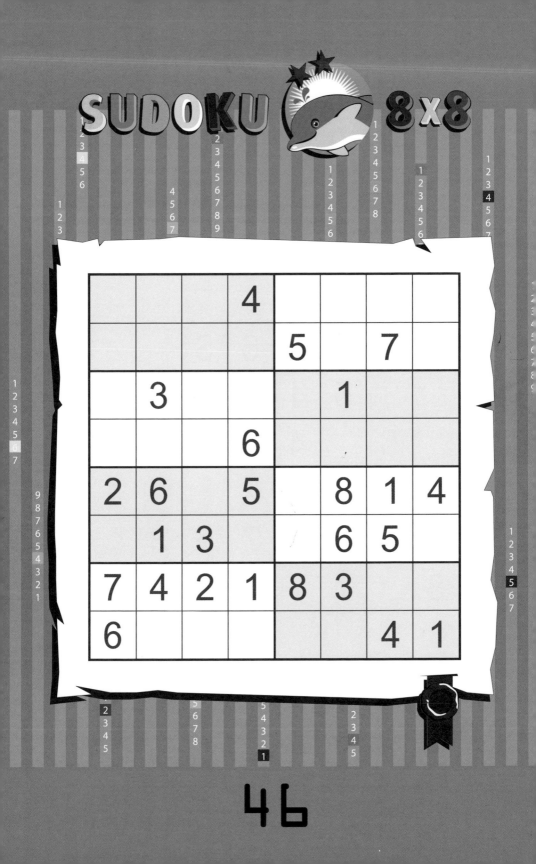

SUDOKU 8x8

46

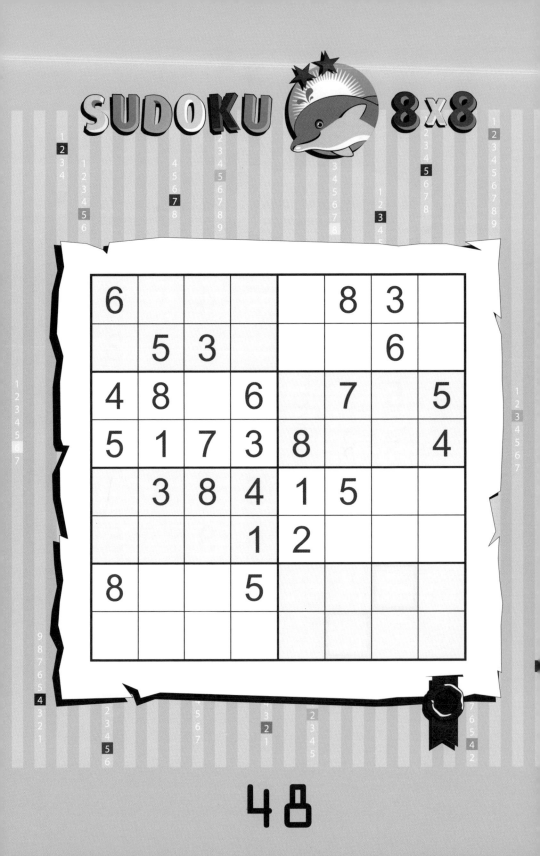

SUDOKU 8x8

6					8	3	
	5	3				6	
4	8		6		7		5
5	1	7	3	8			4
	3	8	4	1	5		
			1	2			
8			5				

48

SUDOKU 8x8

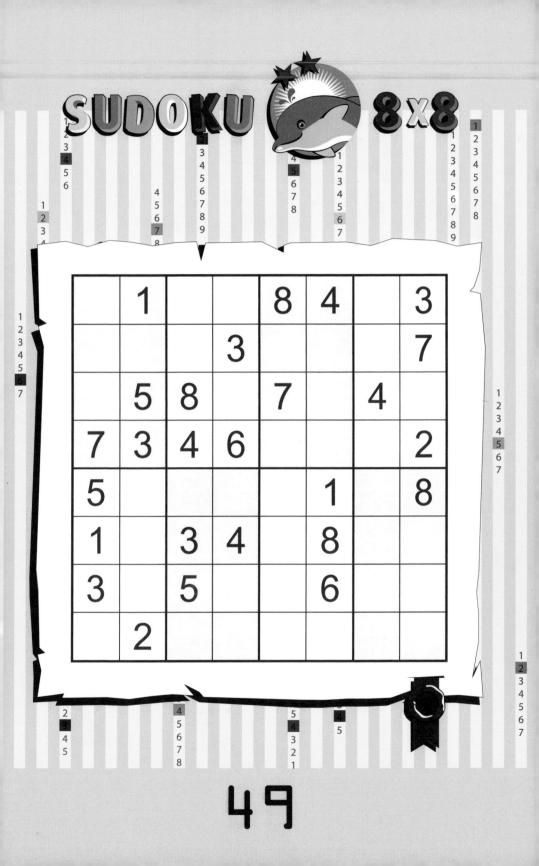

	1			8	4		3
			3				7
	5	8		7		4	
7	3	4	6				2
5					1		8
1		3	4		8		
3		5			6		
	2						

49

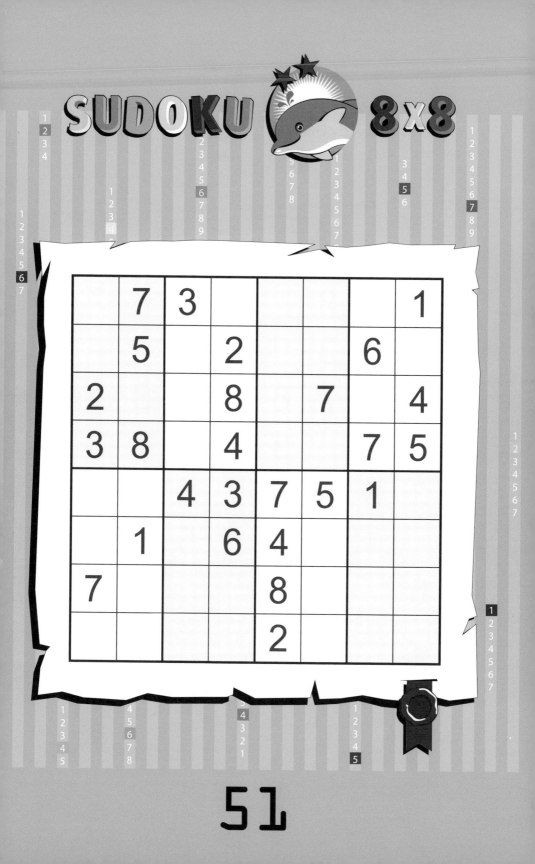

SUDOKU 8x8

	7	3					1
	5		2			6	
2			8		7		4
3	8		4			7	5
		4	3	7	5	1	
	1		6	4			
7				8			
				2			

51

SUDOKU 8x8

2	5	8		4	3		7
		3		1			
5		7	8	2	4	3	
	2		3			7	8
3	8						
	4		6		5		
6						5	
		1					

52

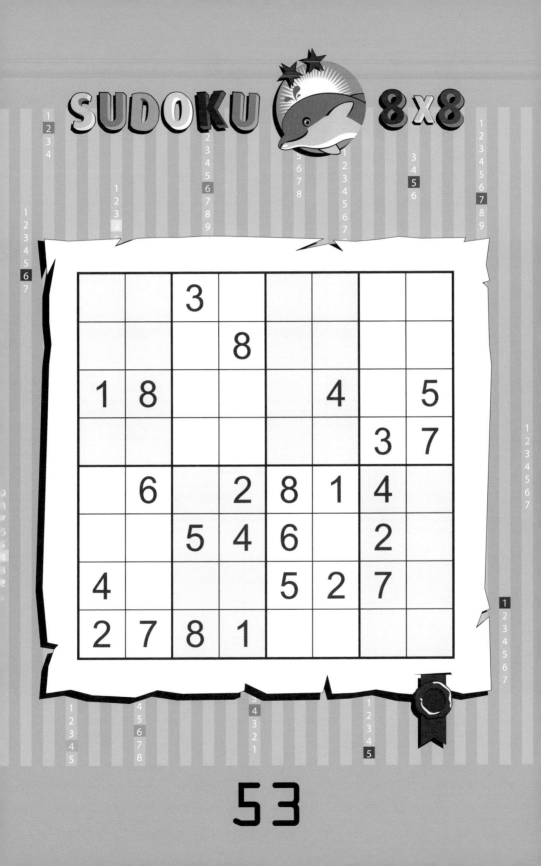

SUDOKU 8x8

		3					
			8				
1	8				4		5
						3	7
	6		2	8	1	4	
		5	4	6		2	
4				5	2	7	
2	7	8	1				

53

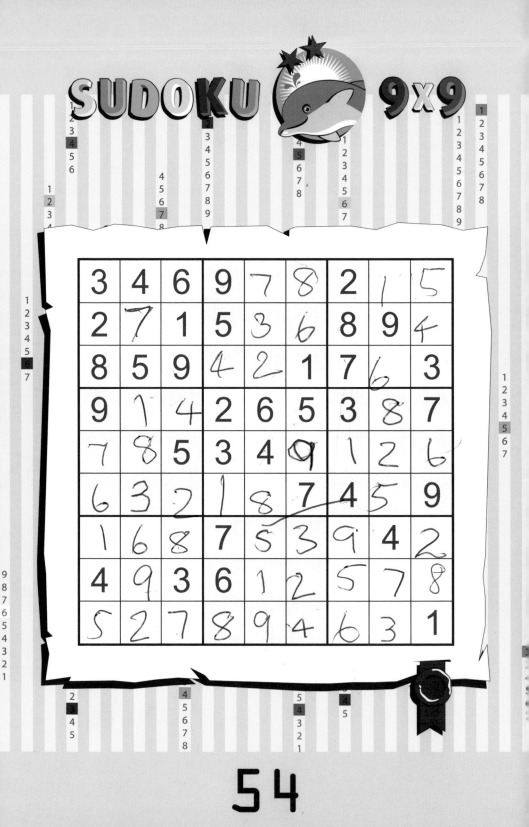

SUDOKU 9x9

54

SUDOKU 9×9

The red ovals contain the sum of the figures in the two connected cells.

55

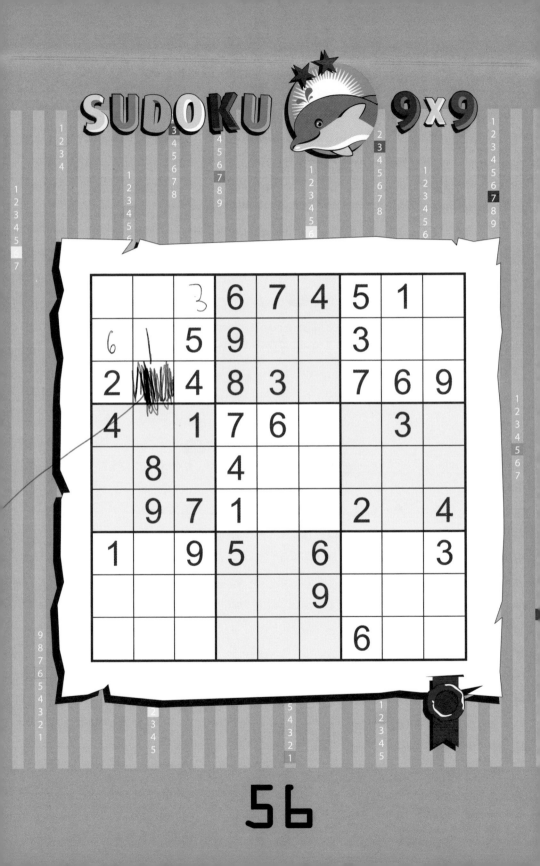

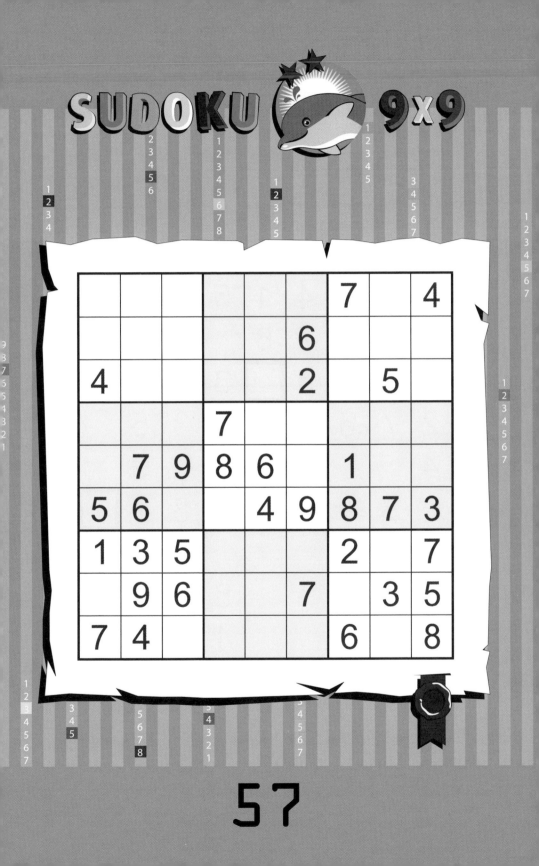

SUDOKU 9×9

						7		4
					6			
4					2		5	
			7					
	7	9	8	6		1		
5	6			4	9	8	7	3
1	3	5				2		7
	9	6			7		3	5
7	4					6		8

57

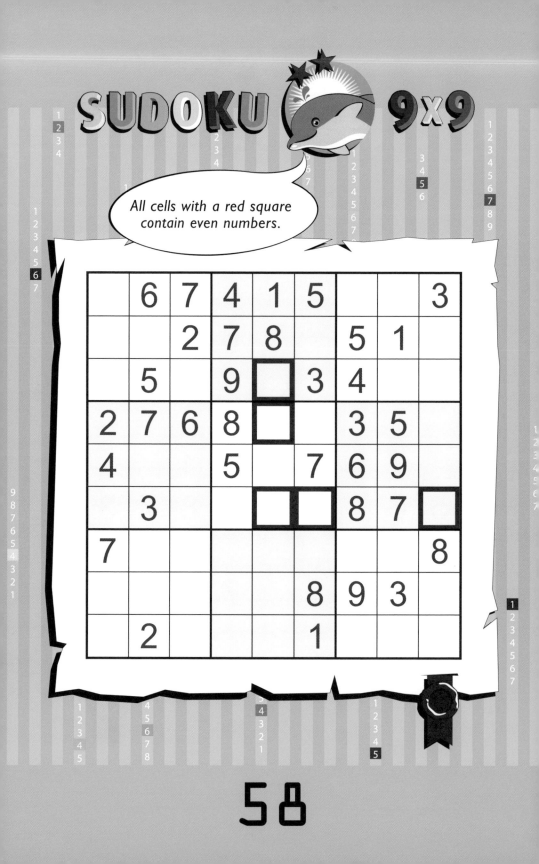

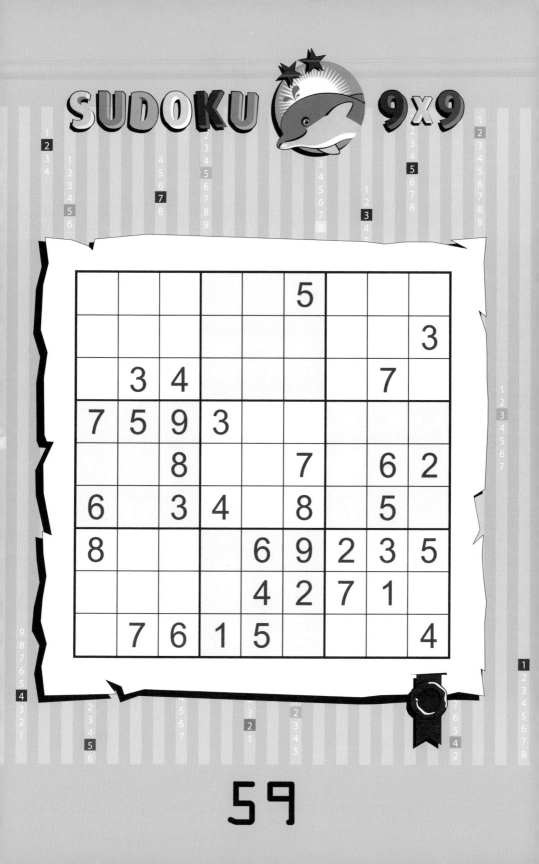

SUDOKU 9x9

					5			
								3
	3	4					7	
7	5	9	3					
		8			7		6	2
6		3	4		8		5	
8				6	9	2	3	5
				4	2	7	1	
	7	6	1	5				4

59

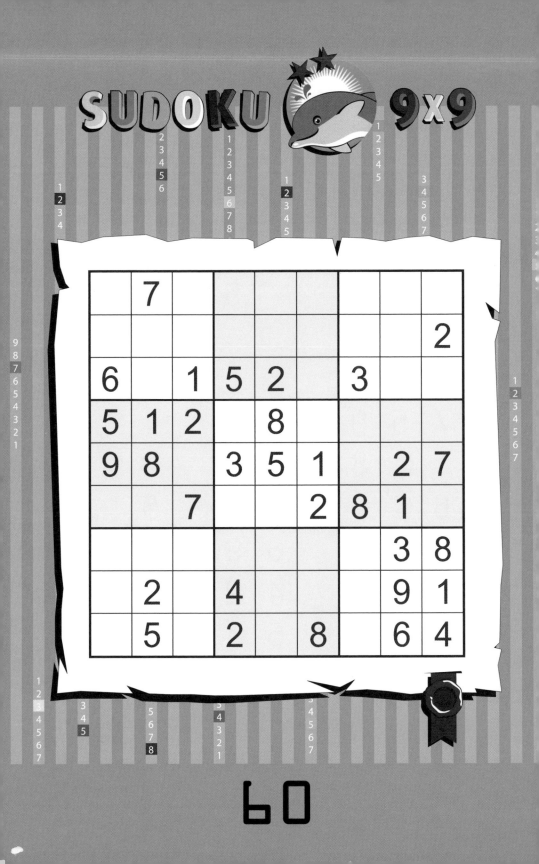

SUDOKU 9x9

60

SUDOKU 9X9

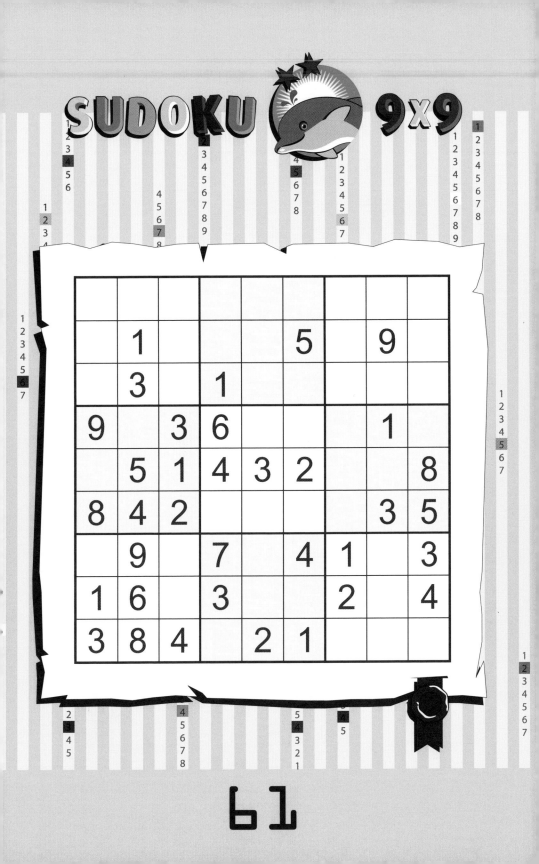

	1				5		9	
	3		1					
9		3	6				1	
	5	1	4	3	2			8
8	4	2					3	5
	9		7		4	1		3
1	6		3			2		4
3	8	4		2	1			

61

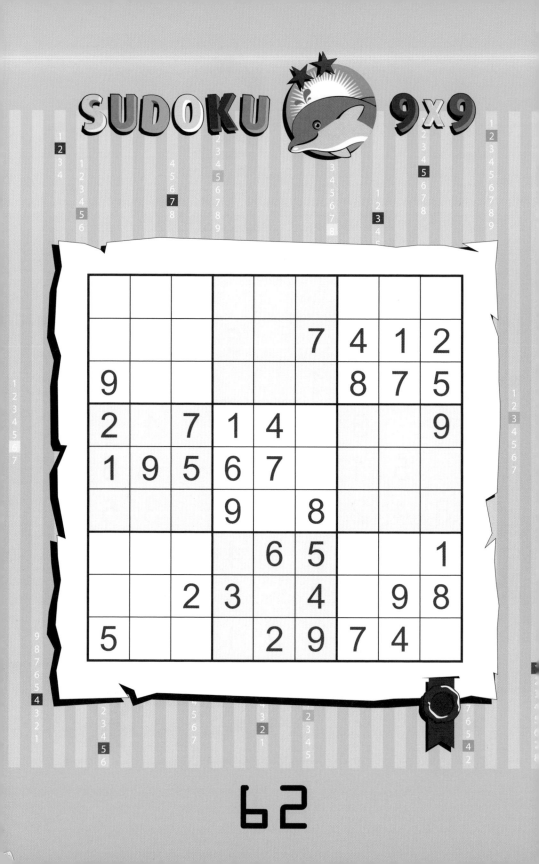

SUDOKU 9x9

					7	4	1	2
9						8	7	5
2		7	1	4				9
1	9	5	6	7				
			9		8			
				6	5			1
	2	3		4			9	8
5				2	9	7	4	

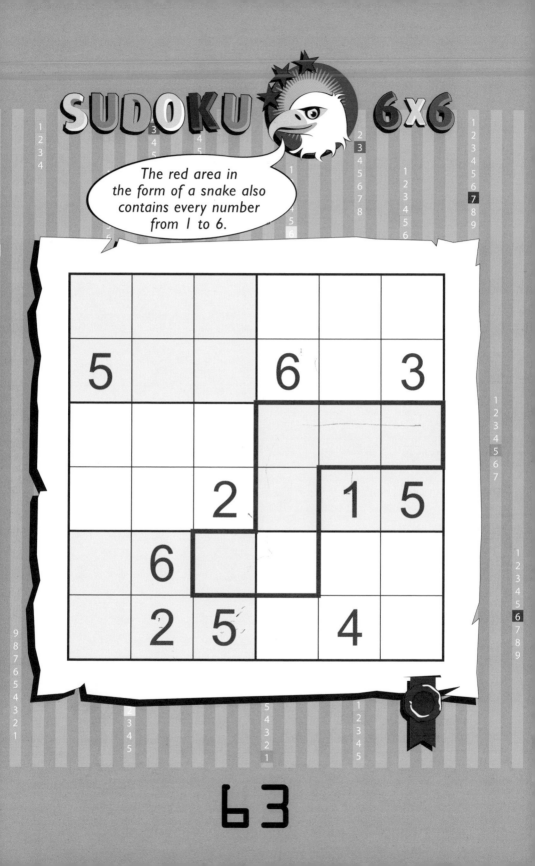

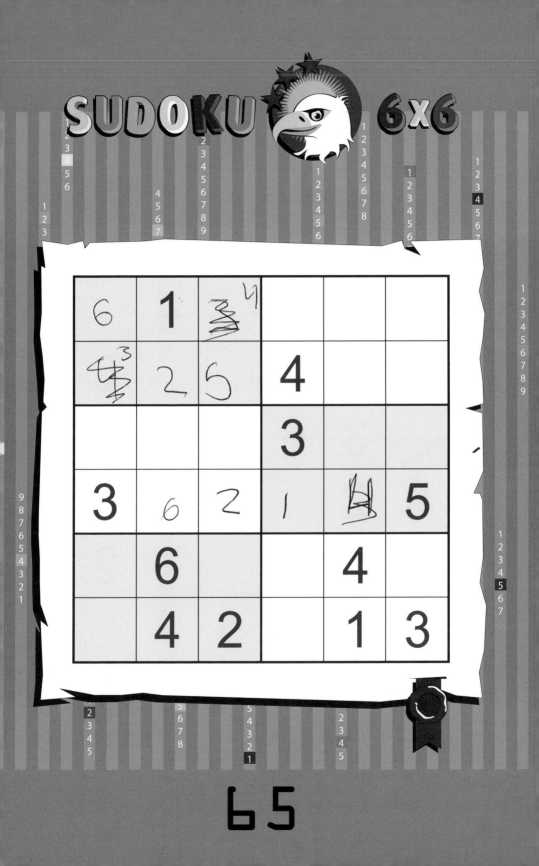

SUDOKU 6X6

6	1				
	2	5	4		
			3		
3	6	2	1		5
	6			4	
	4	2		1	3

65

SUDOKU 6X6

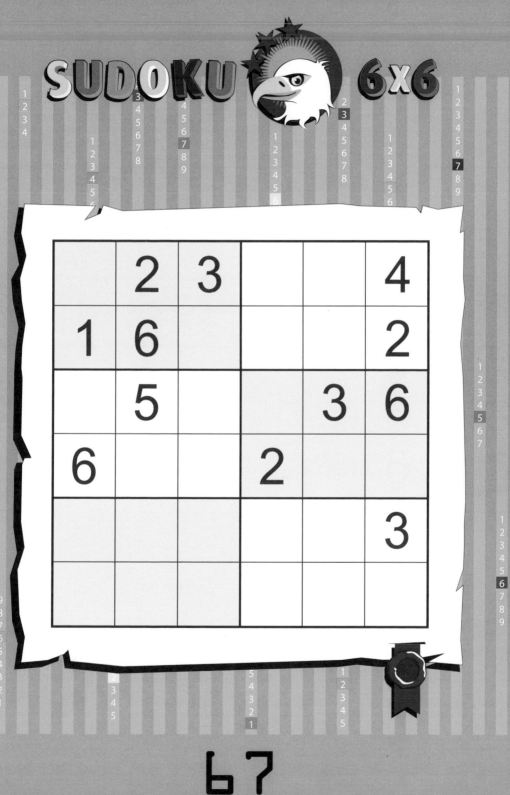

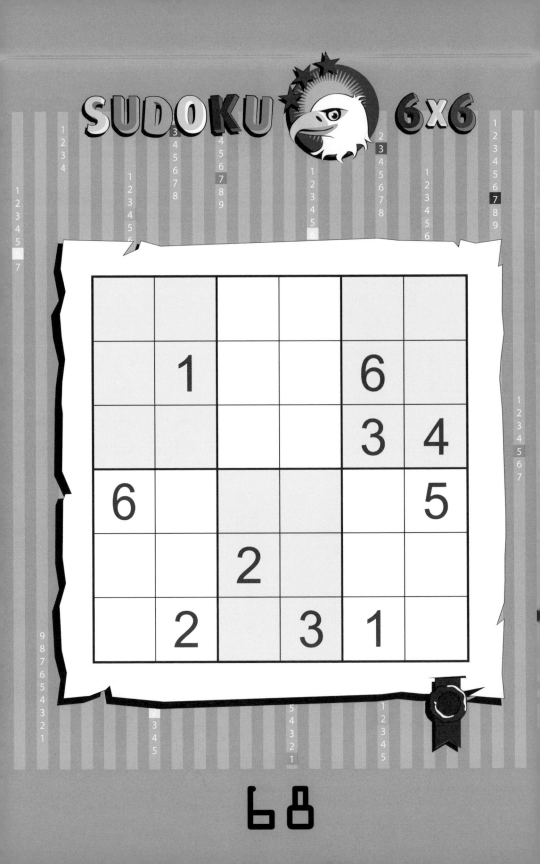

SUDOKU 6X6

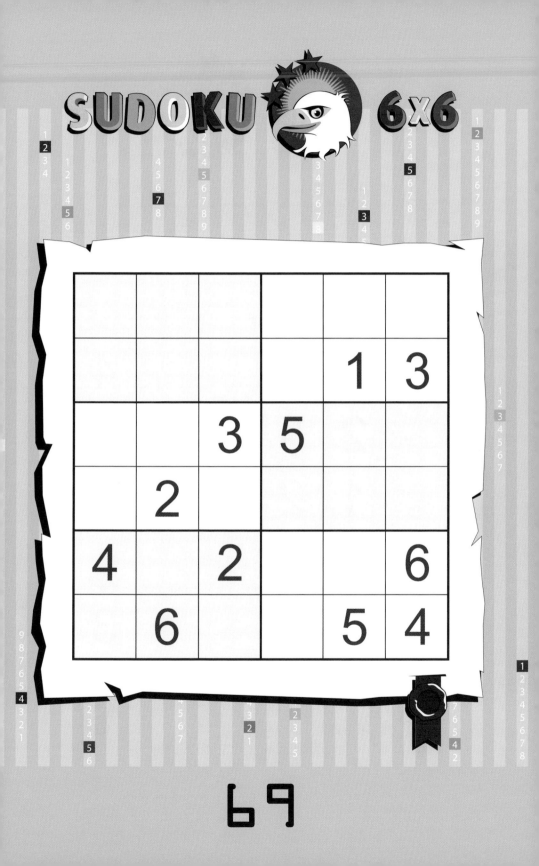

SUDOKU 6X6

				1	3
		3	5		
	2				
4		2			6
	6			5	4

69

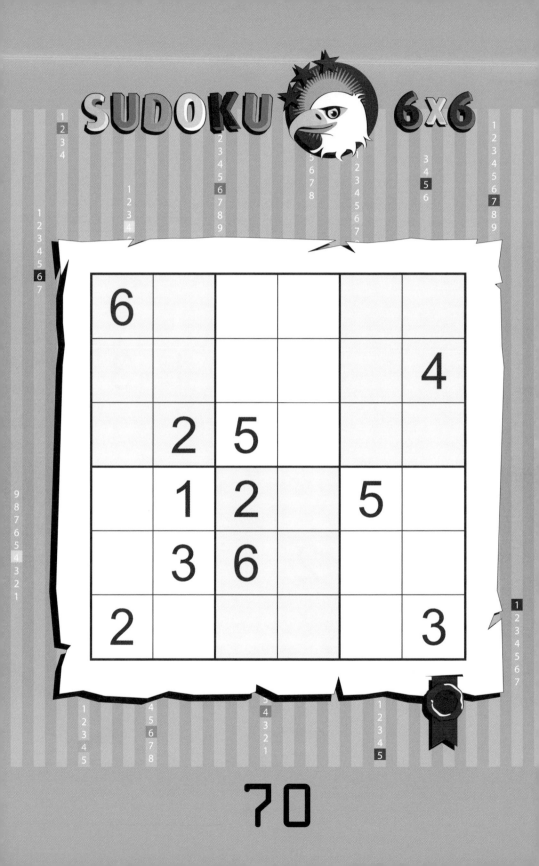

SUDOKU 6x6

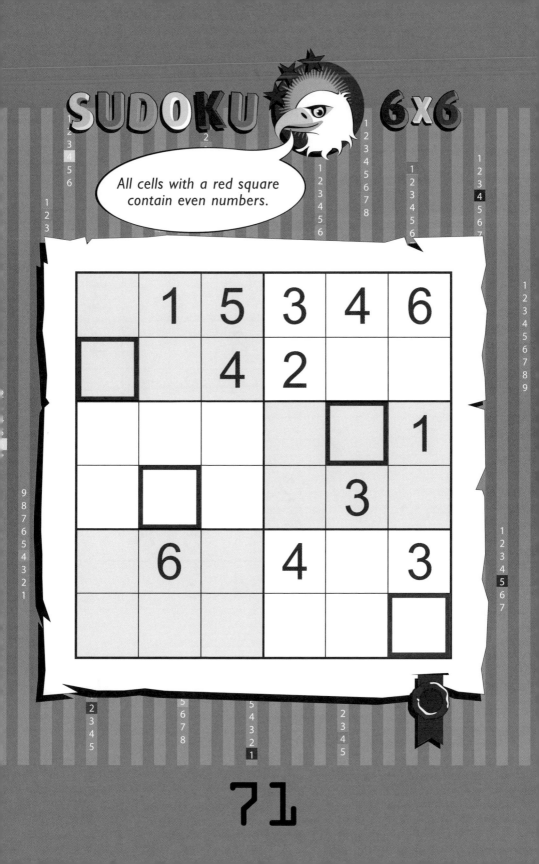

SUDOKU 6X6

All cells with a red square contain even numbers.

71

SUDOKU 6X6

	8	6				1	3
1				6			4
	4			2		7	
7		2			4	3	6
		7	2				
			3		5	8	
				4	3		

72

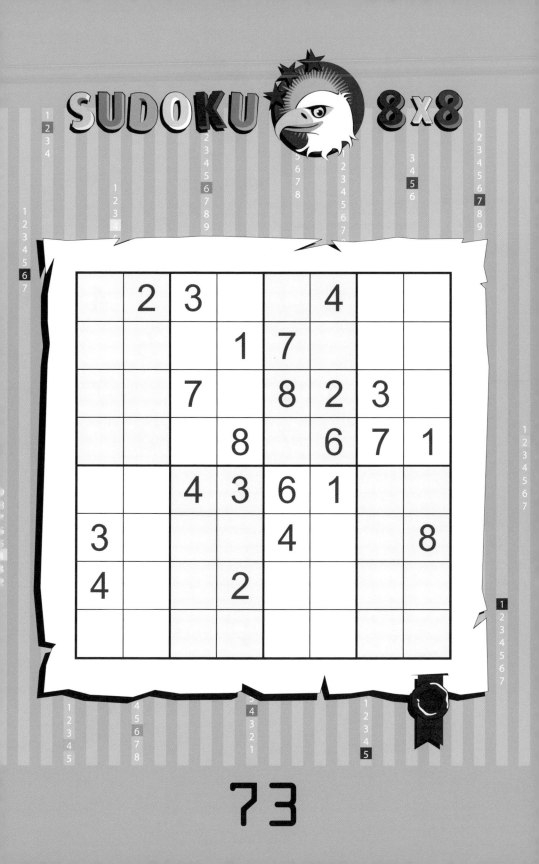

SUDOKU 8x8

	2	3			4		
			1	7			
		7		8	2	3	
			8		6	7	1
		4	3	6	1		
3				4			8
4			2				

73

SUDOKU 8x8

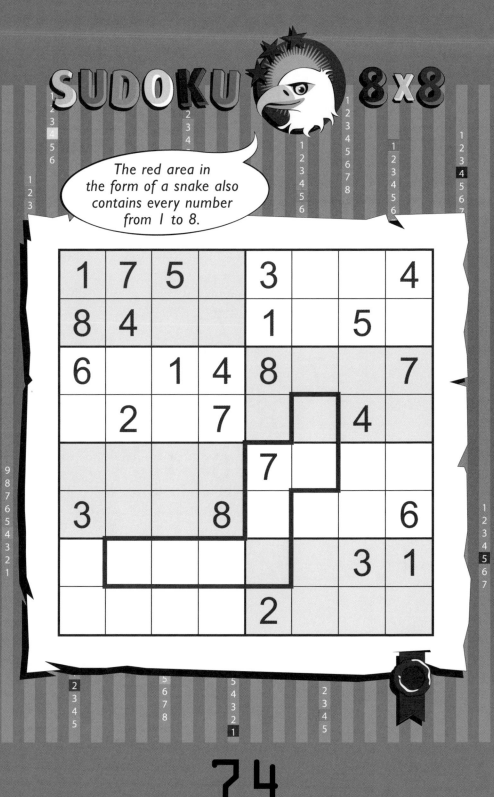

The red area in the form of a snake also contains every number from 1 to 8.

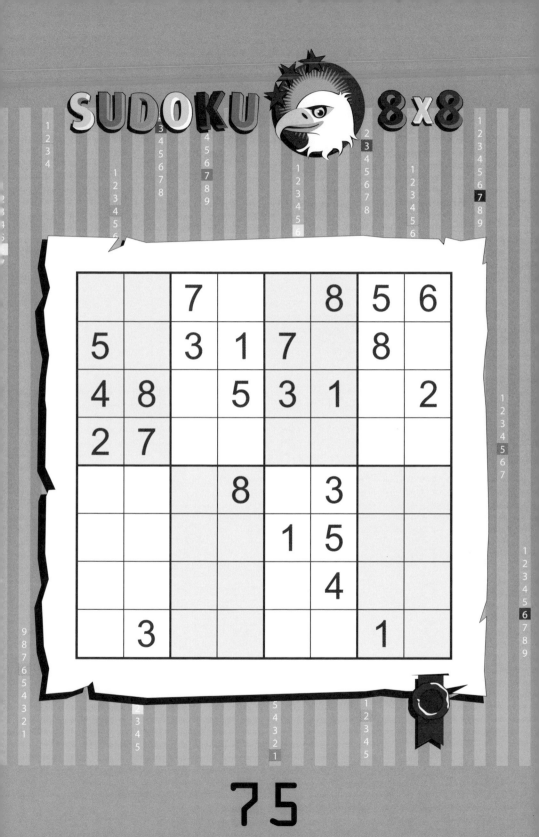

75

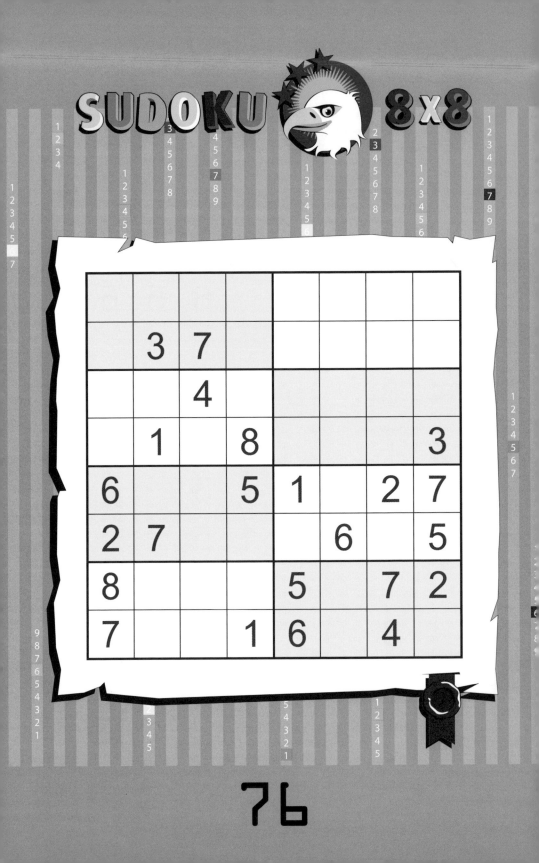

SUDOKU 8X8

	3	7					
		4					
	1		8				3
6			5	1		2	7
2	7				6		5
8				5		7	2
7			1	6		4	

76

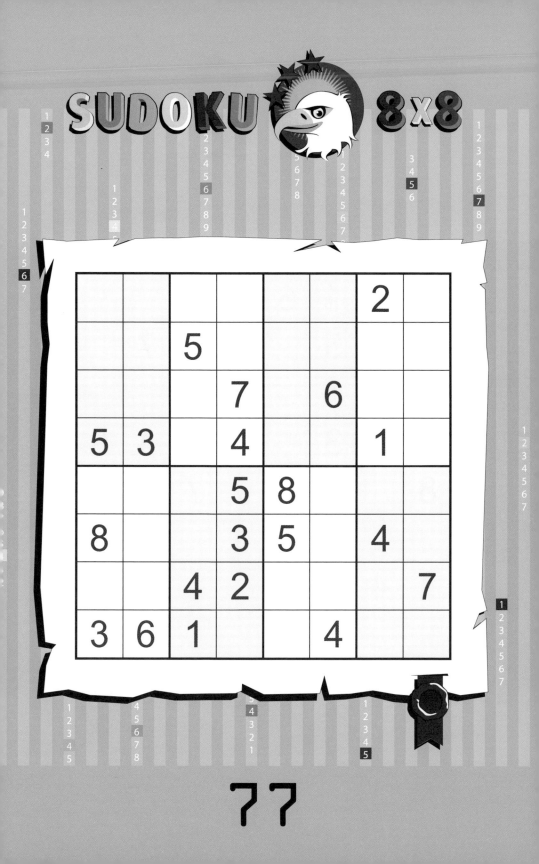

SUDOKU 8x8

						2	
		5					
			7		6		
5	3		4			1	
			5	8			
8			3	5		4	
		4	2				7
3	6	1			4		

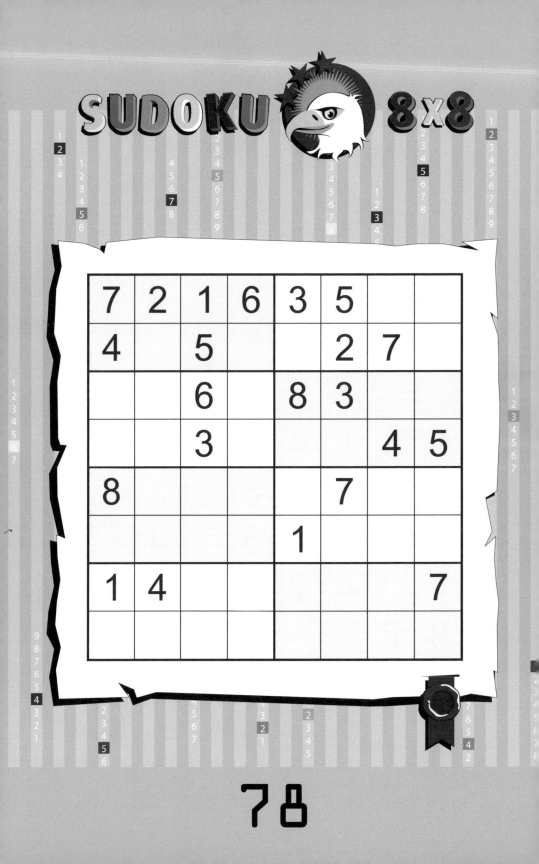

SUDOKU 8x8

7	2	1	6	3	5		
4		5			2	7	
		6		8	3		
		3				4	5
8					7		
				1			
1	4						7

78

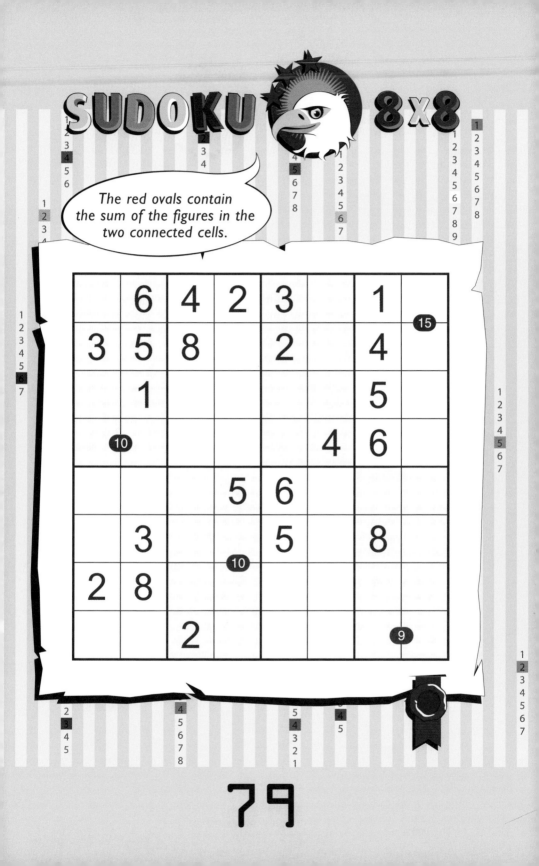

SUDOKU 8X8

The red ovals contain the sum of the figures in the two connected cells.

79

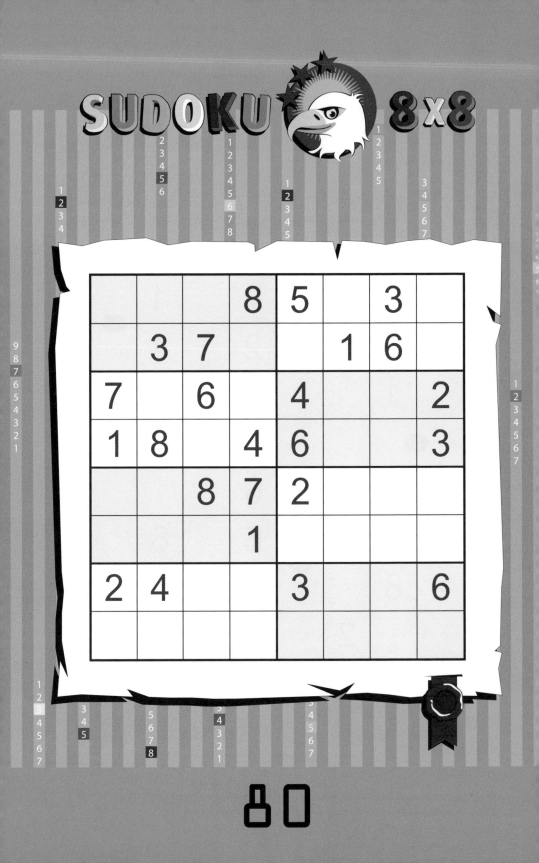

SUDOKU 8X8

			8	5		3	
	3	7			1	6	
7		6		4			2
1	8		4	6			3
		8	7	2			
			1				
2	4			3			6

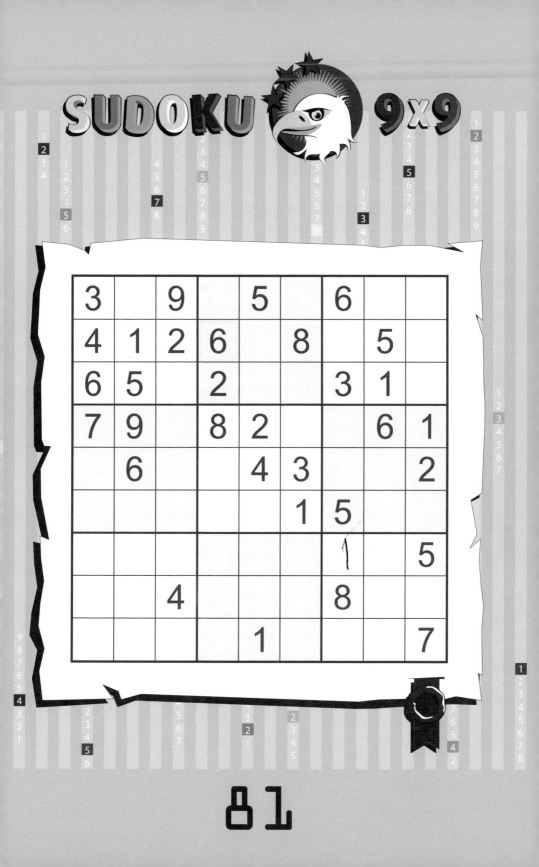

3		9		5		6		
4	1	2	6		8		5	
6	5		2			3	1	
7	9		8	2			6	1
	6			4	3			2
					1	5		
						1		5
		4				8		
				1				7

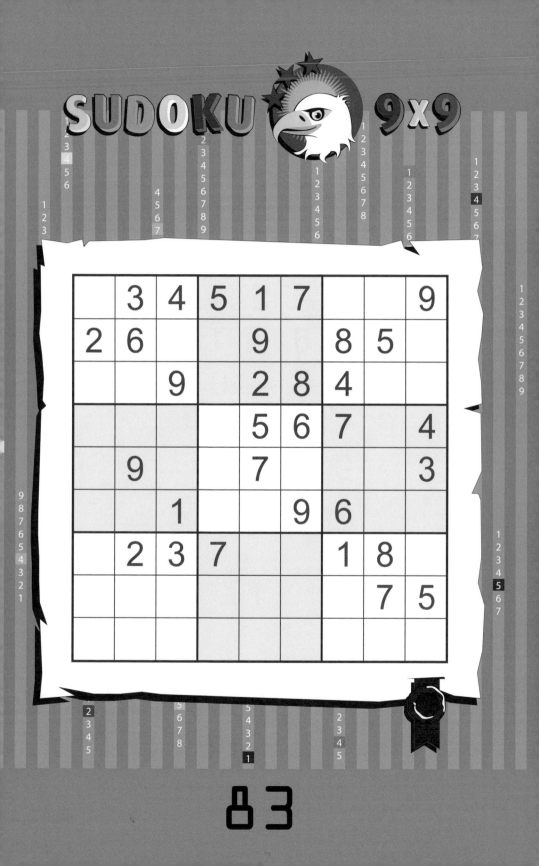

SUDOKU 9X9

	3	4	5	1	7			9
2	6			9		8	5	
		9		2	8	4		
				5	6	7		4
	9			7				3
		1			9	6		
	2	3	7			1	8	
							7	5

83

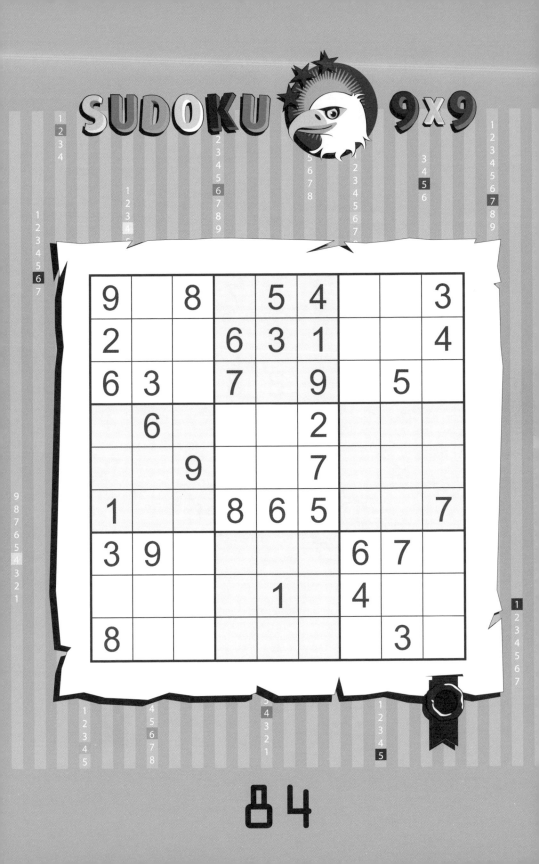

SUDOKU 9X9

84

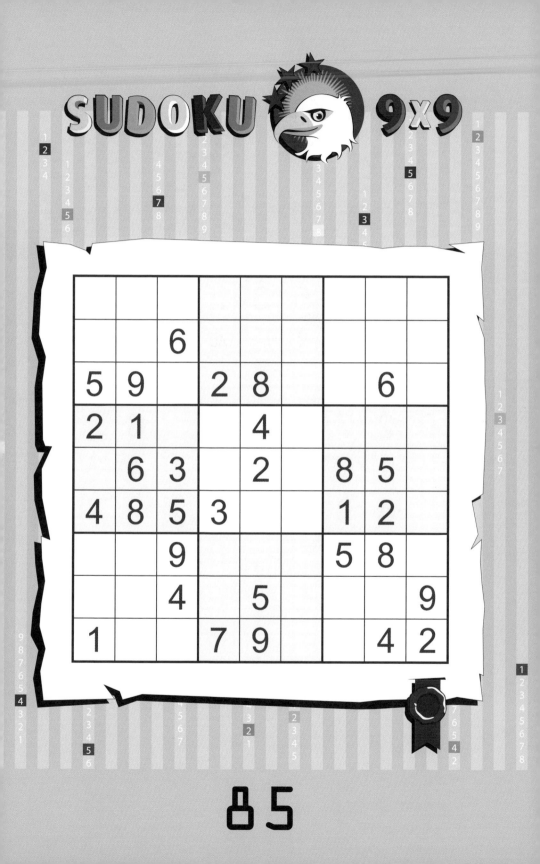

SUDOKU 9x9

		6						
		6						
5	9		2	8			6	
2	1			4				
	6	3		2		8	5	
4	8	5	3			1	2	
		9				5	8	
		4		5				9
1			7	9			4	2

85

SUDOKU 9x9

		8	5	3	2		9	6
	5	9	1		4		7	
4							3	1
9	2	7		4	3		8	
	1			7			4	3
	4	3			9	2		
		4						8
7	9							

86

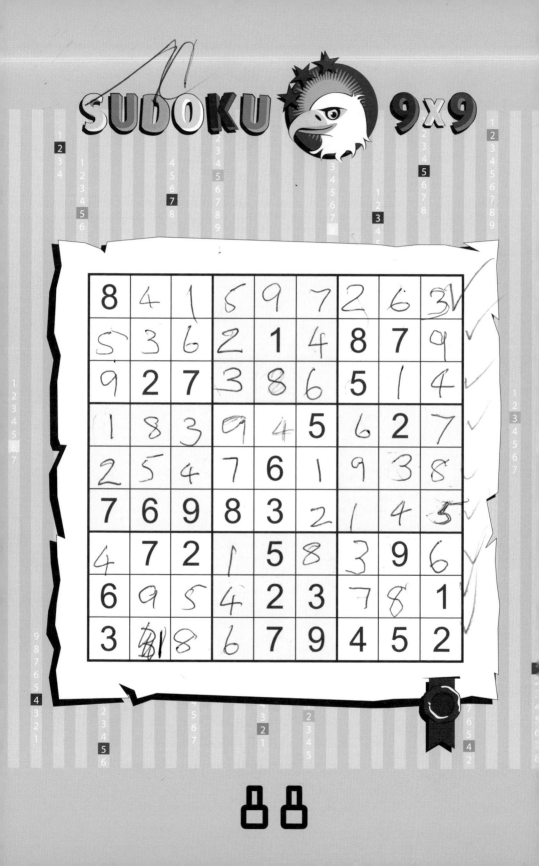

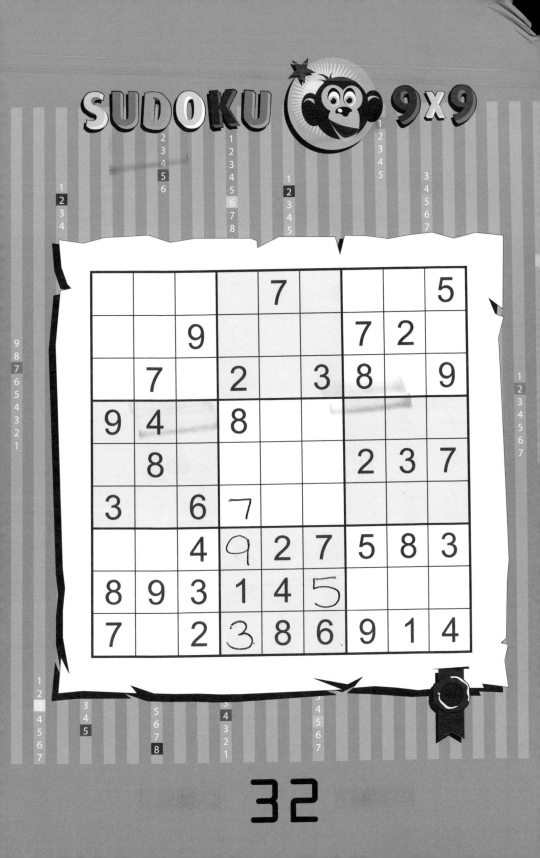

SUDOKU 9×9

				7				5
		9				7	2	
	7		2		3	8		9
9	4		8					
	8					2	3	7
3		6	7					
		4	9	2	7	5	8	3
8	9	3	1	4	5			
7		2	3	8	6	9	1	4

32

SUDOKU 9x9

The red ovals contain the sum of the figures in the two connected cells.

31